FROM BROKE TO BROKER™
How To Turn Your Pain, Pitfalls, and Poverty Mindset into Profit, Power, and Prosperity

DENISE WILLIAMS

www.DeniseTheBroker.com

Book ISBN: 978-0-578-69965-3

TABLE OF CONTENTS

CHAPTER I

HUMBLE BEGINNINGS

My full name is Sha-ta-qua Denise Williams. Yes, I have hyphens in my first name (SURPRISE, SURPRISE). Yes, I was the girl that got picked on because I was given a "ghetto" name. My mother will hate that line because she prefers to call it "unique." She told me she gave me this name because the only other name she could think to name me was Precious.

Well, if you're reading this book, you know that would have been a better fit. However, she was convinced by a hospital nurse to name me Sha-ta-qua because it was so "unique." The funny thing about this is that I have actually worked with two Chautauqua's in my lifetime. It is pronounced the same but spelled differently. Chautauqua has a native American origin. For those wondering what Sha-ta-qua means, I was told at a state fair once that it means Princess. Not sure how true that is or if they just wanted to make me feel good about it.

I went by my first name from elementary school until I graduated from college. When I would list my name as Sha-ta-qua on my resumes, it seemed as if I would never get called back no matter how well put together my resume may have been. However, once I made the switch to Denise, I received more opportunities to interview, and from that point on, I decided it to stick with it.

Things became a little easier for me when I introduced myself as Denise. I didn't have to worry about the awkward silence, the request to spell it, or even sometimes hearing a chuckle or two. Unfortunately, we live in a society where those things matter, and I no longer wanted to allow my work ethic, experience, and top-notch qualifications to be overshadowed by biases and stereotypes. None of those things matter now as much as they used to; however, it has affected how I have presented myself to the world. I am not ashamed of my name; however, strategically and in business, it just makes things a little easier on everyone.

> *Don't focus on the stereotypes.*
> *Focus on your vision and continue*
> *to move forward. Allow your work*
> *ethic speak for itself.*

Growing Up Poor

I was born and raised in Hinesville, GA. It is a small town not far from Savannah, GA. Yes, I am a country girl raised in the South! Hinesville is best known for being connected to the Ft. Stewart army base. My mother was born and raised in Hinesville also and my father is from the south side of Chicago. My parents met because my father was stationed at Ft. Stewart when he was enlisted as an active-duty soldier in the army.

Let's just say that after he met her, he decided this would also be the place he would call home. By the time I was born, my father was no longer an active member of the armed forces. When my parents got together, my father already had three daughters from his first wife. Their names are Zabrina, Terra, and Erica. I am my mother's first child, and I also have a younger brother, Maurice, and a baby sister, Shontiera, which makes me the fourth oldest of six children.

We had little when we were growing up. From today's standards, the house we lived in would have been condemned if the city had anything to do with it. It was an older home with three bedrooms and one bathroom. It was built on top of bricks, so the foundation was elevated from the ground. There were cracks in the window panes, uneven floors throughout, a leaking roof, and small holes in the kitchen floor, just to show you the condition of the home. We would keep it as clean as we could while rotating chores and getting whoopings if we didn't do them like we were supposed to. Even though we were raised on welfare and public assistance, it was important to my parents that we took care of what we had.

I remember being overly excited when the food stamps would come; back then we used to call it monopoly money because of the different colors each food stamp had inside of the food stamp book. Wasting food in our house was a sin! I remember a time when my mother cooked liver for us. Normally, I would look forward to having dinner, but on this night, the food just wasn't good, so when my mother left the kitchen, I threw the food on my plate away.

What I didn't do, however, was cover the food up in the trash can. When my mother returned to the kitchen, she saw the food in the trash can and shouted, "Who threw their food away?" With hesitation, I looked around at my siblings who were all looking back at me and whispered, "I did." After about five minutes of telling me how much she sacrificed to put food on our table, she made me get the liver out of the trash can and eat it anyway. Luckily, it was sitting on the top of the pile, but I will never forget that day. I learned at that moment I should always be grateful for what I have, even if it's not what I want.

My parents raised us the best way they could. My dad worked three jobs simultaneously as a janitor, a dishwasher, and a paraprofessional at a local elementary school. We did not have a vehicle, so he had to ride a bicycle to and from work each day regardless of the weather. My mother did hair inside our home while raising us, so it was a balancing act for sure, but we rarely saw our father; it was as if he was a stranger in our house. We didn't often get to spend time as a family because my father worked so much… not as much as we all would have liked to, anyway. There were really no family vacations or weekend getaways I can remember.

The focus was often to simply make sure that we had all of the necessities of life. My mom did her best to play both roles in my father's absence while he provided for us the best way he could, and I can never take that for granted. I learned my non-stop hustle and hard work ethic from my father. I learned how to be a good woman, have a sense of humor, and my love for Christ from my mother.

Always appreciate what you have, even if it's not everything that you want. Remember, there is always someone that has it worse off than you do.

Childhood Memories

There was never a dull moment while growing up in a household of eight. We would often have company stop by, such as cousins, church family, and friends on the weekends. We would make up our own versions of games, have barefoot races, wrestle, and argue like there was no tomorrow! I remember during our summer vacation, my mother would sign up to be a host for the free lunch program.

The free lunch program was a community outreach program that donated lunches to families in need during the summer while children were not in school. A lot of the children in the community would walk to our house to pick up their free lunch each day. That allowed us to meet even more children, and some are still lifelong friends to this day.

We would all play games outside, such as kickball, dodgeball, basketball, and soccer; you name it and we would play it. We would take the crates that held the free lunch meals and turn them into baseball/kickball bases and basketball goals. We would take old blankets and build tents in the woods next to our house. We build tree houses, and we would climb when my mother was in the house because we knew that we were breaking her rules. We even had a cactus in our front yard, and we would play hide and seek and hide behind the cactus or inside the ditch. At this age, we didn't actually realize that we were poor because moments like these allowed us not to focus on what we didn't have; we were just being kids and enjoying life.

We had a lot of fun, but with that many children and bonus children, things could also get pretty hectic for any parent. My mother was the strict parent and my father was the "yes man." We knew which parent to go to in order to get a yes and which parent would say no. Because of this, I grew up thinking that my mother was the meanest woman in the world! She wouldn't allow us to listen to secular music; she called it the devil's music. We couldn't watch BET, MTV, TRL, or any of those channels in the house. Even some Kirk Franklin songs were banned if they sounded too "worldly."

I grew up attending First Calvary Missionary Baptist Church, where the head pastor is Rev. Sinclair Thorne. He really took his ministry seriously and I learned a lot from him and his family about the bible and how I should live a Christian life. They were great examples of that. My mother was the lead choir director at First Calvary for over 25 years. As a child, at times, I had wished that she weren't because she forced us to attend almost every service that she did, day or night.

On some Sundays, we would even have to attend up to three services and still must go to school on Monday morning. I grew up heavily in the church, singing in the choir, and heavily being involved in the youth program. As a child, I did not understand why it was so important for us to be so active in the church. I mean, other kids didn't have to do all that! But now that I am an adult, those powerful sermons and long prayers have carried me all these years.

Train up a child in the way he should go, and when he is old, he will not depart from it. Proverbs 22:6 NKJV

Break The Cycle

For generation after generation, my family has had to deal with poverty. My mother was a strong woman, and she got her strength from my grandmother. My grandmother survived things I believe would have broken me. She was raised poor, my mother was raised poor, and unfortunately, I also experienced that cycle. Things were not any better on my father's side. It was the circle of life in our family for generations.

As a young child, we would visit our grandmother's house in Buzzard Root on the weekends and during the summer. My grandmother lived on a dirt road on a few acres of land. We would run around barefoot and play in the woods all day and into the night. Her house didn't have a legitimate plumbing system. We had to use a bucket of water from the well to flush the toilet after each use. There was no central heating or air, so we had to use thick blankets in the winter and fans in the summer. I loved going to my grandmother's house because she was the sweetest woman I have ever known. It was like having a little getaway from my parents because I knew that my grandmother loved her grandchildren in a special way. I never knew my grandfather.

My grandmother was the type of person who would give a stranger the clothes off of her back. I witnessed my grandmother give her last to others. Once, she sacrificed her bill money to help a friend in need who just had a newborn baby and did not have the money to pay her light bill. Instead of my grandmother paying her light bill, she gave the money to that friend so her child wouldn't be without lights. A few days later, my grandmother's electricity was shut off. That's the kind of heart my grandmother had. Several years later, she moved from that house and purchased a trailer in the next city over.

My grandmother passed away in her sleep in her trailer when I was 16 years old. The cause of death is still unknown. My mother believes that she died of a broken heart after being let down, struggling and disappointed for most of her life. I was devastated, and when I think about her, I still get very emotional to this day. Oh, how I miss my grandmother, along with her jokes, her hugs, her kisses, her cooking, and her reassurance that God would always provide. I developed my heart to give and my passion for cooking from my grandmother. I love and I miss you so much, Geraldine Jones. Rest in heaven until we meet again!

My mother is also the fourth oldest out of five siblings. She has two sisters and two brothers. Since my father was always working, we did not get to spend much time with him as children. Luckily, my Uncle Rodney, who was my grandmother's baby boy, used to fill that void. He would come over to the house frequently and bring us candy, play outside, and spend time with us. While growing up, I remember being very excited when he would stop by because we knew that when uncle "Hot Rod" was around, we would have a good time, and he would beat up anyone if they ever messed with us.

His personality was contagious, and he was loved by so many people in the community! Everyone knew Hot Rod. Unfortunately, he could not see us grow up for very long… on his way to work one day, he had a head-on collision with another vehicle and died on impact. Even at the young age of 25, our community was shaken by this loss. He is survived by his children, which is a blessing.

The company he worked for, Covan Moving Company, even renamed a street Rodney Jones Lane in his memory and honor, and I learned about the importance of the word legacy from my uncle Hot Rod. Like him, when my time on this earth is done, I want to leave such an impact on others that people all over the world remember my name. I love you and miss you, Uncle Rodney! Rest in heaven until we meet again!

To my angels, I promise to make you both proud! I love you.

CHAPTER II

GROWING PAINS

Middle School Was A Nightmare

I attended Hinesville Middle School (aka HMS) in the sixth and seventh grades. I used to walk to and from school every day. I would meet up with some of my childhood friends a couple of blocks away and we would finish the route together. The community helped raise us, so we would walk without worrying about being kidnapped or robbed. One advantage of growing up in a small town is that we had a family member on every street. However, when I started middle school, life became real.

I was picked on quite a bit in middle school. Some of the kids that I met in middle school were not kind at all. My level of awareness that I didn't have a lot of what the other kids had become more apparent. I used to wear hand-me-downs, my body was slow to develop, I had bad acne from puberty, and the worst part of it all was that I had a crooked smile. I was very embarrassed to smile showing my teeth. So much so that any picture you see of me during this time, I was smiling without showing any teeth. I struggled with self-confidence, and I call this my ugly duckling phase of life.

HMS must have been an old motel turned into a school as each classroom comprised one to two motel rooms. You even had to go outside to go to the restroom, the cafeteria, the gym, and even the principal's office. During lunch, we could go to an area outside called the Outback. The Outback was where boys would chase girls, students would catch up on the latest gossip to find out who was dating, and where fights would break out occasionally. This was every student's favorite time of the day, hands down!

One day, I had one of the most embarrassing experiences of my life. I had a group of five best friends, and we would always eat lunch together every day. Well, that group of friends soon became a group of mean girls. One night, I was on the phone gossiping about one of my best friends. I believe I said on the call I really didn't like her that much. The next day, when I arrived for lunch, all of my best friends were already sitting down eating because they had gotten there a little bit earlier than I had.

When I got my tray and came to sit down in my normal seat, as soon as my butt hit the chair, they all stood up in a synchronized fashion and left me there to eat alone. I was so sad and embarrassed that I cried. I had no idea why they would do me this way! I later found out that I was set up on the call as a three-way call and the girl who I was talking about was on the other end! I felt so betrayed! I was then banished from my girl group of friends for a while. Eventually, we reconciled our differences and became friends again.

Luckily, I also had other friends I made on the cheerleading team and track team, but this was definitely a memory I will never forget. It taught me that at any moment, what you say not only can be recorded, but it can be used against you. Also, I learned to be careful who I confide in and share my business with, and that trust is at the core of every relationship you make. I honestly do not know if HMS was up to building code based on today's standards. Since then, it has been torn down, but its memory still lives on. I was transferred to Snelson Golden Middle School in my eighth-grade year and that is when I met my best friend, who is still my best friend to this day.

High School Was A Whole New World

My father finally found a full-time job with benefits and my older siblings graduated from high school successfully, so my family's financial position improved. I was grateful to move to a different home because, by this time, I was 13 years old. Things were finally turning around. We moved to a new three-bedroom, two-bathroom house inside a subdivision, which was a lot nicer than our first home.

However, since I had a little brother, he got to have his own room while my baby sister and I shared one. I hated that I still did not have my own room or my own privacy. I had to share a room and sleep in a bunk bed until I graduated from high school.

Through that experience, my passion for real estate intensified. I promised myself as I laid in my bunk bed that one day, I would own a mansion so big that I would not even know that other people were there. To date, I still have that same goal and I am 100% certain that it shall come to pass.

Before I attended high school at Bradwell Institute (better known as Bradwell or BI), I got braces, my skin cleared up, and I became a beautiful young woman. During high school, I continued to be highly active in sports, I became the captain of the cheerleading and track teams, I participated in beauty pageants, and I had leadership roles in different clubs. I also got my first job at Winn-Dixie. My cousin was the manager, so I started working at 15. I was excited about having my first job because now I started making my own money. I did all of this while also maintaining the A/B honor roll.

I started "feeling myself." Since I was making good grades, and overall, being a fairly good child, my parents allowed me to date. I dated and I had my first experience of relationship drama. Despite the emotional rollercoaster I experienced between love and heartbreak, I was still able to graduate at the top of my class, be appointed as the senior class treasurer, and receive the women's athletic scholarship for track and field.

However, I hung up my cleats after high school because, by then, I was burned out after running consistently since the age of five. Overall, I really enjoyed my high school experience and I would not change a thing. I really learned the power of organization, time management and the importance of juggling multiple responsibilities at once.

I have always been an overachiever as some may call it, but I just call it ambition.

CHAPTER III

GOOD GIRL GONE BAD

Moving Out

I graduated from high school in 2006 and decided that I wanted to attend a university. My mother recommended Savannah State University (SSU), but I felt it was just too close to home. However, I wish I would have had more insight and knowledge about HBCU's because I probably would have given it a shot. I could have also gone to the University of Georgia (UGA), but I was too nervous to move that far away from home, and I was terrified of driving on the interstate. Instead, I attended Valdosta State University (VSU) in Valdosta, GA. I was far enough away for my mother to have to call before she came, and Valdosta State did not have a track team, so I felt it would be a perfect fit.

When I received my acceptance letter, I was very excited and could not wait to move in the Fall. I still remember my first day at freshmen orientation. The upperclassman put together a full itinerary. We were given a tour of the beautiful campus, a breakdown of the different programs that the school offered, and the history of the school. I met some amazing individuals on my first day. I absolutely loved the campus overall, as well as the programs that the university offered.

What I also loved about VSU was that they allowed freshmen to live off-campus. That was a big deal for me because I knew that I could finally have my own room!

I secured an apartment off-campus but within walking distance of the school, which was great. As a bonus, I shared my monthly expenses with a childhood friend from Hinesville, who also attended VSU. We shared a two-bedroom, one-bathroom apartment with a small kitchen, but I loved it because, for the first time in my life, I had my own privacy. I never lived on a college campus or in a dorm room.

Little did we know that we were renting an apartment on a street that was infamous for throwing college parties... BOOOOOONE DRRRRRIVE! It was a street full of members of Greek organizations, football players, and other college students. There was no shortage of parties on Boone Drive.

I am naturally a social butterfly, so it did not take long for me to make more friends. We shared a lot of experiences between cookouts, college parties, club events, campus events, etc. We partied frequently and I was really enjoying my college experience. I even joined an on-campus modeling group during my freshman year, which was a real dope experience. However, no matter how much we stayed out, I would always make sure that I went to class, completed homework, and maintained my HOPE Scholarship.

There is nothing wrong with enjoying life; however, don't lose sight of your goals. One simple mistake can cause you a lifetime of pain. Trouble is easy to get into but hard to get out of... Wise words that my mother would always share with me.

Rumor Has It

One day, while on campus, I met a young man who I will call DB. He was a junior and I was a freshman. Soon, we hung out and started dating each other exclusively. DB was the type of person who lived life on the edge. He lived a life without regrets and had somewhat of a bad boy persona, whereas I lived a life that was a bit more sheltered and risk-averse. We were like fire and ice. He was well known on campus, so I met a lot of friends through him and since he was also a party promoter, I was able to go out often without paying a dime.

Needless to say, we were living young, wild, and free. When my mother met DB, she felt he would not be a good fit for me. She did not dislike him as a person, but she warned me about his character. As a young woman, I defended him and stayed with him because I felt like she did not know what she was talking about and she was too judgmental. I brushed it off, even though I knew that she only wanted what was best for me. Soon after that, I would hear news that shook me to my core.

I was a server at Red Lobster and a coworker of mine approached me during my shift and asked me if I had heard about a rumor going on around campus? I was caught off guard by the question and asked him what he was talking about? He replied that a mutual friend of theirs told him that DB got a girl pregnant. My initial response was that he was lying and there had to be some sort of mistake. He seemed 100% certain, so I told my manager I was not feeling well and needed to be let off of my shift. I was released and went home early so I could get to the bottom of this. I did not want to have this conversation over text message or over the phone, so I asked DB to come over to my place.

When he got there and I saw him, I was immediately enraged! I told him about what I heard, yet he denied every bit of the rumor. I threatened to break up with him, but he still denied this rumor had any validity. After yelling and crying for hours, we both eventually calmed down and I agreed to trust his word on the matter. However, something about this situation was still very unsettling. I reached out to the woman that the rumor was about. I went to her place and asked her about what I had heard.

Of course, she told me that the baby was DB's. I was devastated, but I was also still in a state of denial because I wanted to trust what he had told me. I mean, there is no way he would lie about something like this, right? I gave him another chance but told him he would have to get a paternity test and if the child was his, then we were done.

For the next couple of months, things were still very rocky between us, but we were trying to make it work. I really did not share the news with many people because I was too embarrassed about what was going on, and I also hoped that he wasn't making me look like a fool on campus. So, I just did my best to put that in the back of my mind and keep moving forward.

Several months later, something about my body felt different. I remember the morning I woke up and decided that I needed to take a pregnancy test. Reluctantly, I drove to the nearest Dollar Tree and purchased a pregnancy test; however, when I made it back home, I decided to wait until the next day to take the test because I was extremely nervous about the results.

The next morning, when my roommate was gone, I decided to bite the bullet and take the test. The pregnancy test showed a strong positive result and I could not believe it! I was breathless. I remember falling to my knees and crying profusely. Crocodile tears poured from my eyes and my heart was pounding so hard that it felt like I would have a heart attack. I stayed in the bathroom for another hour as I contemplated my next move.

I remember some of the questions that were racing through my mind during that moment. I asked myself, "Do I tell him?" "Do I keep it?" "Do I abort it?" "What is my parent's going to say?" "What are my friends going to think about me?" "Do I drop out of school and move back home?" "How am I going to afford raising a child?" "Why did this have to happen to me?" I mean, I was a good church girl, with a bright future and rarely got into any trouble before I got to college. This just did not seem fair.

After speaking with DB about it over several conversations, we decided to keep the baby. It did not take long before the word spread like wildfire across our campus, and I spent weeks feeling sorry for myself and wondering how I could have been so stupid. Now, two of us are pregnant by the same man, at the same time, on the same college campus. I was so embarrassed that I allowed myself to be in this situation.

Love is blind, if you let it be. Trust your gut and protect your heart.

You're On Your Own

A few months went by and it felt like the entire college campus knew about my pregnancy and now, so did some of my family members. I told my father, but I could not build up the courage to tell my mother and I begged him not to tell her. I avoided going back home to visit for as long as I could, but I knew that I could not hide forever. It had been a while since I visited home and my mother kept asking me to come home to visit. I finally agreed to come home, but this time, I asked DB to come with me so we could let her know together.

Well, things did not happen as planned. One thing that my mother loved to do when I visited home was go shopping at Rainbow, Citi Trends, and It's Fashion. Those were our spots! As I got dressed to go shopping, I did my best to hide my stomach. I literally changed outfits three or four times before I finally landed on a black shirt and some jeans because I heard that black makes you look slimmer. While we were at the store, she asked me to try on a few outfits and let her see how they looked, which is our normal routine when we are out shopping together. Well, I agreed to try them on, but I never came out to show her how they fit. About 30 minutes later, we were ready to check out.

I put my clothes on the register as she stood to my left side and had a full side view of my stomach. I was about five months pregnant and I still had only a small pudge, but my mother knew. While standing at the register, I will never forget her words: angrily, she said, "You done went out and did what I told you not to do, didn't you?" I just stood there like a deer in headlights and said nothing. Then, she told me I could pay for my own clothes or put them back because she was not paying for them. Sad and embarrassed, I went to put the clothes back on the racks because I did not have enough money to buy all those clothes.

As we left the store, my mother could not even look at me, so instead of having the sit-down discussion we had planned, we headed back to Valdosta that evening. The next day, I received a call from my mother expressing how upset and disappointed she was in me; however, the call did not last long... the true purpose of the call was for her to inform me I was cut off. She let me know that they would no longer be supporting me financially and that I would need to figure things out on my own. I was disheartened and upset.

Even though I knew that I was wrong and that being pregnant was not an ideal situation, I never thought I would be neglected by my mother when I needed her the most. I felt abandoned and I was heartbroken, sad, angry, and lonely.

This was a pivotal moment in my life because now, I was forced to grow up and figure out how to take care of myself independently, and my pregnancy was far from easy. My mother and I did not speak for months after she found out. I was still taking college classes, being judged by some of my peers, and trying to pay all of my monthly bills on my own. I contemplated terminating the pregnancy multiple times because I was so unhappy. A few months later, the paternity test results were in and DB was the father of the other child. At times, the stress of it all would cause me to fall into weeks of depression and anxiety.

There may have been times in your life that you did not make the best decisions. However, don't allow those challenges to stop you from realizing your greatest potential.

Pregnancy Troubles

As my son grew inside me, I did my best to embrace the journey and make the best of it. I found another job in customer service, so I did not have to stand on my feet all day. However, I was still going through so much at once those moments of happiness were few and far between. All the things I was going through weighed heavily on me daily, so much so that at work one day as I sat at my desk, I felt lightheaded. Moments later, I passed out and hit the floor due to high blood pressure.

My manager called the ambulance and I was immediately rushed to the hospital. When I woke up, I was in a state of panic because I thought I would lose my baby, but luckily, that was not the case. The doctor let me know that he was okay but that I was really stressed and overworked and that I needed to eat better and get rest. They gave me fluids and gave me a note recommending that I would need to be on bed rest for about a week. That incident made me realize that I needed to protect this life in my womb and that I needed to focus on getting him into the world safe and sound.

Little did I know that the bad news during my pregnancy had just begun. A few weeks later, I went in for a normal check-up when I learned that something was abnormal about my ultrasound. Neither the ultrasound tech nor the OB-GYN would confirm with me exactly what was going on. Instead, I was told that I would need to see a specialist in Atlanta, GA, right away.

They set up our appointment for the following week and I was anxious to find out what was going on with my baby. During the ultrasound appointment, I was told that my son had cysts growing on his lungs that were potentially fatal. I instantly burst into tears! No mother carrying a child ever wants to hear that there is something wrong during their pregnancy. I began to blame myself and feel like a failure. As a first-time mother, I did not know if this would lead to other issues, such as developmental delays, down syndrome, etc. All I knew was this was not the news I wanted to hear. After learning I had a high-risk pregnancy, I knew then that I needed my mother. I called her and let her know the disappointing news. We both shed tears during the call and reconciled our differences that day.

Due to the complicated nature of his condition, I was also told that I could not have him in Valdosta because there were not any specialists there who could handle his delivery if he needed immediate surgery. Because of this, I could not have a completely natural delivery. Initially, his due date was on Halloween, which was October 31, 2008, but instead, I was scheduled to be induced on October 15, 2008. There was a total of five doctors and nurses in the delivery room with me as we awaited my son's arrival, and no one really knew what to expect.

By the grace of God, my son was born the following day, on October 16, 2008, and he cried as soon as he entered the world, which was a sign he could breathe! Everyone was excited to hear him cry, and he was taken out of the room immediately and placed in the Newborn Intensive Care Unit (NICU) for further testing and observation.

Life is too short to hold grudges. We must learn to forgive one another. None of us know how much time we have on this earth. Do not leave it with hate in your heart. Forgive.

Destined for Greatness

It was nerve-wracking seeing my son poked and tested all day and night. Due to his condition, we had to stay in the hospital for a week before we could be released. They wanted to monitor his breathing until they felt comfortable that he could breathe easily on his own. They gave me general instructions about his care and gave me a breathing treatment machine to bring home with us. Until the day before his release, I did not have an official name for my son. I had to solicit family and friends for help, and finally, we decided on the name Destin because he is destined to be here, and he is destined for greatness!

When Destin was three weeks old, we had to bring him back up to Atlanta for another check-up. What we thought would be a normal check-up just ended with another round of bad news. While the nurse was listening to Destin's chest with a stethoscope, she said nothing, and the room had an awkward silence. I watched her move the stethoscope around his chest frantically, as if she was not hearing what she thought she needed to. She quickly excused herself without explanation and left the room.

A few minutes later, she came back in with a doctor and I knew then that something was not right. All I could think was not again! I felt a sharp pain in my stomach because I was so terrified of what they might say. I finally built up the courage to ask, "What is going on?" The doctor looked over at me and said, "You will not be able to take Destin home, he will need to be admitted into the nearest hospital immediately!" As a new mother, I did not know all the signs to look for and I was unaware that something was seriously wrong with him. I felt like I had failed him, again!

Destin was not getting the proper oxygen that he needed, and he was struggling to breathe. Once Destin was admitted into the hospital, we were told that he would have to have surgery the following morning. I was told that during the surgery, the doctor would have to cut him open to remove half of his left lung and remove any other cysts that might be present. I was horrified thinking about Destin having to have serious surgery at such a young age.

All of this happened without warning, so I was not prepared financially, nor did I pack enough to stay in Atlanta for the weeks ahead. I was just a young, broke college student on Medicaid, and I was not sure what I was going to do.

Fortunately, the hospital told me to contact the Ronald McDonald House of Charities for assistance. The RMDHC took me in, fed me, gave me a room, and provided a 24-hour shuttle for me to visit my son any time of day or night for free while he recovered from surgery! Their organization operates on donations primarily, and I had nothing to give. However, I knew that I would never forget what that organization had done for me.

After Destin's surgery, my son was almost unrecognizable. He was swollen from the surgery during the first couple of days. He had tubes hanging from his side to drain the blood, oxygen tubes in his nose, and because he was so little, the only place they could put the IV in was his forehead! Watching Destin recover from surgery was one of the hardest moments of my life! Seeing my son go through the pain of being pricked and cut open while fighting for his life is a moment I will never ever forget. I would not wish this moment on anyone.

As I sat by his side every day and night, I began to self-reflect, pray, and plan for our life ahead. I promised my son I would do everything that I could to protect him, provide for him, and support him for the rest of his life. Watching his strength gave me strength, and together, we would make it through this. About a month later, we were discharged again from the hospital and I am blessed to say that Destin is a healthy, intelligent, and handsome young man. I could not be prouder to call him my son. In hindsight, I now understand why my mother was so protective of me. A mother never wants to see their children hurt or in pain in any way. There is nothing like a mother's love. We are now best friends to this day, and she is the best grandmother in the world! I love you mama.

To Destin & to my unborn children, I promise to do everything that I can to make sure that you are protected, provided for, and prepared for what this world may bring. I rebuke every generational curse from our family. Going forward, we will leave a powerful legacy that will be honored for generations. We are favored by God and covered by his grace. Amen.

Mama, I Made It

Due to missing so many weeks of school because of Destin's surgery, I had to apply for incomplete grades in each class that semester. Instead of being on track to graduate in four years, at best, it would take me five years to graduate. This all happened in my sophomore year in college, so I still had a long way to go to get to the finish line. But I returned to school as a single mother, determined to finish my degree program by any means necessary.

This was by far one of the hardest moments in life for me; trying to raise a son, while working a job, going to school, and paying my own bills. However, I was laser-focused on getting to the finish line. I was committed to not becoming a college dropout or just another statistic. I would go to class and go to work during the day, and I would do homework and study for tests in the middle of the night. Sleep was a luxury but getting to my goal was a necessity.

I would not allow myself to make excuses or blame my child for what I could not achieve because of becoming a young parent. I continued to stay active on campus and I was inducted into the Beta Gamma Sigma honor society for Finance and Accounting majors. I maintained my HOPE Scholarship, and I pledged Delta Sigma Theta Sorority, INC!

In May of 2011, I graduated with a bachelor's degree in Finance, becoming the first person in my family to graduate from any College or University. I was so proud of myself to have overcome so much and still leave Valdosta State with a degree in hand. I know that I could not have made it across that stage without God's grace and without the village that helped me with Destin throughout my college career. Thank you to my parents, my siblings, the Berrian family, my college friends, my line sisters, my daycare providers, etc. I appreciate you all from the bottom of my heart. I could not have done this without you.

I had to walk across that stage to show other young women and men that it's possible. Getting that Finance degree was bigger than me. I hope that this has inspired someone else to finish the program that they started! Don't give up on YOU!

CHAPTER 4

WELCOME TO THE REAL WORLD

This Can't Be My Life

After graduating from Valdosta State University, I had to decide where I wanted to live. I knew that I did not want to stay in Valdosta, and I did not want to move back to Hinesville, so I took a leap of faith and relocated to Atlanta, GA. At first, it was rough because I did not have a specific plan in place. I was putting out applications, but I was struggling to find a decent job. My cousin was dating a young woman who worked for TitleMax. She told me about a job fair they were having, so I attended and was hired for a position. However, I still did not have a place to live, so my cousin allowed me to sleep on his couch for about a month, and when I got my first check, I found a cheap apartment on the southside of Atlanta and moved out.

I was grateful for the opportunity with the company, and in less than six months, I was promoted to an Assistant Manager position because I worked as much as I possibly could to take care of myself and my son. However, I hated going to work each day. Not that I did not like corporate America, but some of the company's practices did not align with my morals and ethics.

We would repossess vehicles from people who had been paying on their loan for years, sometimes 3x over, but since they only made the minimum payment, it only applied to the interest and nothing towards the principal balance.

There was a "no grace period policy." If a client was late on their payment even by one day, I used to have to leave the office and go into the field in my personal vehicle, go to the customer's house, and call the office to send a tow truck if I spotted the vehicle. That job was extremely dangerous. The last straw for me came when elderly customers would come in to make payment arrangements because they were living off social security checks and begged us not to take their vehicles. I could not take it anymore; I would leave work distressed and feeling guilty that I was taking advantage of people.

When I would go home and self-reflect, I could not understand why it was so hard to find a decent job. I did everything I thought I was supposed to do: I went to college, I graduated with a business degree, I pledged in a sorority, I had over 100+ community service hours, and I had a high GPA. I knew that I was overqualified for some of the positions that I was applying for, but for some reason, I was still not good enough for employers to give me a chance.

That was when I realized that I had to take my life into my own hands. I could not allow others to dictate my worth. I got online and searched for jobs that would allow me to make millions or even billions! Real estate seemed to be a consistent industry that came up and it was already one of my first choices. It was an industry that would allow me to have the flexibility I needed as a mother, the opportunity of unlimited income potential, and the ability to look cute at work every single day! Yes, being cute matters. I took it a step further and studied the world's richest people... they all owned real estate! At that moment, I told myself, this is it!! THIS IS IT!!!!

When you know your value, it causes you to have crazy faith! Do not stay in a situation that does not align with your morals and values. Always stay true to yourself and eventually the money will follow.

One Degree Wasn't Enough

I was excited to have identified my purpose, but when seeking new business opportunities, you must take the good with the bad. Although real estate is a very lucrative industry, it is also extremely volatile. I read articles and watched videos about what happened during the real estate crisis that began in 2008. It was 2012 and we were finally recovering from the market crash. This showed me I could not put all my eggs into one basket.

Therefore, I obtained my real estate license in July 2012, and the following month, I started classes to obtain my MBA degree at Clayton State University. This way, if, for some reason, the market tanked again, I could find a job in corporate America and my family would not lose everything and have to start over from scratch. I knew that I did not want to ever be poor again, so I did not want to be too risky.

As I attended CSU, I had little time to be as active on campus as I would have liked. The workload was unreal! I was balancing being a parent, being in a relationship, working as a Realtor and Agent Services Coordinator simultaneously for one of the largest real estate firms in the world. It was the perfect opportunity to work in my field while pursuing my graduate degree. Fortunately, I was able to close deals between classes.

In this role, I saw how the company was run from the inside out. I helped plan company events, answered phones, onboarded agents, assisted with recruitment and retention, etc. What really inspired me during this role was how much money the firm was making. I was in an office with over 200+ agents. Commission checks would come in daily, and the name of the agent on each check would change, but one name that remained on every check was the brokerage's name. That was when it hit me! I was focused on being on the wrong side of the industry. I knew that I needed to become a Broker so I could have leverage. From then on, I was on a mission to learn as much as I could about the real estate business from a Broker's perspective.

The workload in my MBA program seemed to be a lot more demanding than it was in undergraduate school. It required a lot of sleepless nights, long nights in study groups, and time away from friends and family. I remember that I used to literally go to sleep in my car at work sometimes rather than eat because I was so exhausted. I worked and went to school seven days a week for two years straight because most of my classes and/or study groups were held on the weekends. However, I knew that I had only two choices: either to graduate or to graduate. I did not allow myself to have any other options. You can't deposit excuses!

My favorite part of the MBA program was that it allowed students to study abroad. I studied abroad during both years of my MBA program. During the first year, I studied abroad in the country of Panama. I experienced sailing on a boat through the Panama Canal, we visited several Fortune 500 companies with offices in Panama, we ate the amazing cuisine, toured some historic sites, and experienced the nightlife. I had a blast in Panama!

In the following year, I studied abroad in China. We stayed in both Beijing and Shanghai. This was the furthest I had ever been away from home. China was an incredibly unique experience for me. While I was there, I visited Tiananmen Square, silk markets, Fortune 500 companies, the Alibaba headquarters, universities, and the Olympic stadium, also known as the "Bird's Nest". I even faced my fear of heights and climbed the Great Wall of China. I did not complete it, of course, but I did ride the slide back down the wall. The night tour in Shanghai was magical. Seeing the architecture and the lights at night was a delightful experience.

I felt like a celebrity while I was over there because everywhere that I went, the local people wanted to take photos with me, touch my hair, and skin. At first, I was a bit uncomfortable, but I just embraced the moment and went with the flow. The experiences I had in China were experiences I will never forget.

Attending CSU and graduating with not one but TWO MBA degrees is one of my proudest moments in life! I obtained an MBA in International Business as well as an MBA in Supply Chain Management/Logistics. I not only walked across the stage with two degrees, but I graduated Summa Cum Laude with a perfect 4.0 GPA! I was inducted into Beta Gamma Sigma: The International Business Honor Society for being ranked in the top 1% of my class. This was an amazing achievement and writing this brings tears to my eyes.

Dream BIG! When you think you can't, you then can't. If you think you can, you WILL!

I Do or I Don't

After graduating from Clayton State University, I was sought by several great companies for employment. I decided to give corporate America one more try since I had just earned additional degrees and would continue to work my real estate business as well. In my corporate role, I was Port Logistics Manager and I oversaw multiple ports on the West Coast. The role had many great benefits such as paid travel, a health/dental package, and retirement/investment accounts. I would fly to San Francisco, Oakland, Portland, Seattle, and LA. Life seemed like it was finally on the right track, I now had three college degrees, I was earning a great income, and I got engaged to be married. I honestly believe that this role is the perfect fit for someone who enjoys inventory management. After testing the waters, I knew that real estate was still my passion.

My fiancé worked in sales and was one of the top salesmen in his company. He was asked to relocate to Jacksonville, FL. I was a bit nervous to move out of state, but to compromise, I quit my corporate job and agreed to relocate to FL as well under one condition. The agreement was that I would receive the support I needed to pursue real estate solely.

While in FL, I went back to real estate school to obtain my Broker license. I then joined a dynamic real estate team. I did my best to find happiness in being in a new city with no friends or family and embrace the new lifestyle, but things got rocky in my relationship. We faced unreconcilable differences and I decided to call it quits and move back to Atlanta.

At first, I was very embarrassed and ashamed that my engagement failed. We had already started planning the wedding, posting photoshoots on social media, and planning for the future. I had moved away from friends and family to be with him, just to have to move back to Atlanta and start my life all over again. I know there are people who stay in relationships because they do not want to be embarrassed in the public eye.

Well, I figured it was better for me to leave during an engagement rather than end a relationship years later in a divorce. I had to put my happiness first and do what I felt was best for me and my son regardless of the judgment I had to endure by others. I harbor no ill feelings towards him to this day; however, sometimes, you must follow your gut, and since then, I have never looked back.

I'm no relationship therapist, but I am a strong believer in being happy and knowing my value, even if that means having to start over from scratch.

Failed Partnerships

When I moved back to Atlanta, I partnered with a start-up real estate firm and was brought on as the Associate Broker for the company. When I joined the team, there were less than 10 agents on the roster and the company did not yet have office space. In that role, I assisted the Qualifying Broker with recruitment and retention, marketing, agent training, systems, etc. I really poured my heart into that role and worked extremely hard to help grow the firm.

During my time with the firm, I helped the company grow to over 65 agents, open an office space, purchase investment properties, build vendor partnerships, sell millions in real estate, and more.

I worked in that role for less than two years before an industry professional noticed my hard work and approached with an opportunity to start my own firm as a joint venture. At first, I was reluctant to accept the position, but I knew that in my current role, there was a cap on my ability to grow, so I submitted my resignation letter.

The company we started was called Love & Williams Realty. This was my first real estate brokerage and it failed shortly after take-off. I was caught up in the excitement of starting my own company, putting together marketing campaigns, and making more money. However, I failed to do my due diligence with the partner I worked with. Since we were brought together by a mutual friend, I trusted that everything would work out well. It did not take me long to realize that my partner had no intention of holding up her end of our agreement. As time passed, it became clearer that I was sharing 50% of the revenue with a person who was not matching that with 50% of the effort. After a few months into the business, I gave a written notice I wanted to terminate the business partnership.

Well, a few days later, I received an email from the company's accountant stating that unauthorized funds had been drafted from our company's bank account. My initial thought was that it was hacked because real estate companies are at a high risk for wire fraud. I was shocked to find out that it was not a stranger who took the money, but my very own partner! She not only transferred thousands of dollars into her personal LLC, but she paid her rent and Georgia Power electric bill from the company account as well. I was very hurt and confused. I contacted her immediately and gave her a strict timeline to return the money, but she did not.

The next day, I filed a police report and a complaint with the Georgia Real Estate Commission. A few months later, we had our day in court, but my business partner was a no-show. I presented my case to the judge, along with documentation and receipts, and the judge found her guilty of theft by taking, and based on the amount taken, that crime is considered a felony in the state of GA. On top of that, since she failed to appear in court, a warrant was issued for her arrest.

I honestly never wished it had to go that far. We should have been able to work together as women and as business partners, period. We could have easily dominated in the marketplace and positioned ourselves to make a lot of money together! This was a very unfortunate situation, but I remain hopeful that all partnerships will not end this way. For those of you reading this and are considering starting a business with a partner(s), I encourage you to do your due diligence, ask for receipts, make sure that proper documentation is in place, and plan your exit strategy if things don't work out.

Strong, well-written shareholder and operating agreements are the prenups of the business world.

CHAPTER 5

BET ON YOURSELF

Dust Yourself Off and Try Again

I was TIRED! I was tired of dealing with disappointing setbacks in my life over-and-over again. I was getting discouraged, and that is when the self-doubt started to sneak in. I remember telling myself that maybe I was doing too much, I was not experienced enough, no one would support my business anymore, I couldn't afford it alone, what if the next one fails too, etc. Being transparent, I was terrified to try again! I gave myself a couple of days to cry it out and think through my next move. After speaking with close family, friends, and some of the agents on the L & W team, they encouraged me and gave me the confidence to start over again. They reminded me I was already doing it, but that I had been doing it for someone else. They backed me 100%, so I gave it another try.

Williams & Co International Realty was approved as an LLC on May 15, 2018. I officially opened the brokerage to hire agents on June 1, 2018. I was now the 100% shareholder of my own real estate brokerage firm, making me one of the youngest real estate Broker/Owners in the nation! I opened my firm with no investors, no partners, no grants, and no backup plan. Williams & Co is a self-funded business and I am immensely proud of that. It all happened because of God's grace coupled with unstoppable grit and determination.

Many people do not know the magnitude of this accomplishment because they do not understand the difference between an agent and a Broker. As an agent, you cannot work independently, you must affiliate your license with a Broker who must agree to hold your real estate license. You do not have to become a Broker at any point in your career and most agents never do for many reasons. Out of the agents that do obtain their Broker license, often, they still work under another Broker as an Associate Broker or a Team Leader. Rarely do they start their own brokerage firm or open a real estate franchise.

There is no right or wrong way to run a real estate business. Frankly, owning a brokerage is not for everyone. The skillset that it takes to be a successful agent differs completely from what is required once you become a Broker. As the Broker, you have leverage because every transaction that closes by every agent on your team technically belongs to you. Therefore, the brokerage firm receives a percentage or fee from every transaction that closes under the brokerage firm. As a Broker, you are responsible for recruiting, compliance, overhead expenses, marketing, and the list goes on.

Selling real estate is cool, but my passion is training, personal/business coaching, event planning, and systems. That is why I became a Broker. I enjoy seeing other agents get their first client, I love seeing smiles on agents' faces when they get their first commission check, I love helping them get through difficult transactions and seeing them get better at negotiating and closing. I genuinely believe in pouring everything that I have into my team. Just like with anything else, the higher the risk, the greater the reward. It is truly rewarding to have an elite team of agents to help me build this brokerage powerhouse.

Sometimes you must create your own lane. If I had let self-doubt stop me, then Williams & Co would not exist today. Run towards the fear, and when you overcome it, you will be glad you kept fighting!

If You're Going To Do It, Do It Right

The first office space I had for Williams & Co was in Atlantic Station. I negotiated to have the lease roll over from Love & Williams Realty into Williams & Co's name and take over the lease. Well, halfway through the lease, I received a letter from the property management company stating that the office space provider I was leasing my suite through lost their contract with the building. Because of this, every tenant that used that space provider had less than 30 days to vacate their suites.

I was so disappointed because I really enjoyed the location and the office environment, and now my team was without an office. Meanwhile, I was permitted to host my training classes at the office of one of our preferred closing attorneys' locations, not too far away. This helped; however, soon after that, the closing attorney's office closed their doors, and once again, I had to go back to the drawing board.

I got a membership at a co-working office facility and hosted company meetings there. Since it was a members-only based facility, the only time I could meet with agents or for agents to meet with clients is if I was there with them. As you can imagine, that caused a huge inconvenience for all parties. This went on for several months as I worked to save on overhead expenses; however, it caused the company to slow down its growth rate.

I was interviewing agents frequently and they loved what my company offered but did not like we did not have an official office space. After being turned down by several top agents, I realized that if I was going to do it, I needed to do it right!

I planned and prayed long and hard about growing my firm. I knew that an office space would be a long-term commitment as well as a large overhead expense because what I wanted was going to be expensive. After searching and touring several office spaces and comparing locations, amenities, suite sizes, prices, etc., I found exactly what we needed. As soon as I walked into the office lobby, I knew I had to have it!

There was more negotiating and back-and-forth that took place that almost made me lose faith we would get approved for the suite. But, by God's grace, we were approved for an office space in the Lenox Towers building on the 16th floor on Peachtree Road, which is considered Buckhead's original address. Buckhead is a very prestigious and affluent area in metro-Atlanta. I could not wait to move in and share the news with the team!

This is a prime example of what you call a "Minor setback for a major comeback!" Never lose faith.

No, It's Not Easy

During my real estate career, I have closed millions of dollars in real estate through residential, commercial, and investment transactions. I have trained and hired over 100 agents as Broker between firms. I also donate thousands of dollars to non-profit organizations each year (the Ronald McDonald House is one of my charities of choice).

I am extremely proud of what I have been able to accomplish in this incredible industry, but it has not always been glamorous. I have had days when I would come home and cry myself to sleep because I felt like the world was on my shoulders. I have had moments when I had more expenses than income. I have endured the disappointment of having friends support other companies in the same industry. I have dealt with people spreading false rumors or talking negatively about me behind my back. I have been taken advantage of by vendors paid in advance for work that was never done. I have had to let agents go because their ethics did not align with mine. The list goes on and on. So no, this decision to start my own company has not been easy.

I have been approached on several occasions by other firms offering to merge and/or buy out my firm and we would work under their company. I was awfully close to making that decision twice. Both times, the opportunities sounded amazing and like it would benefit all parties; however, once the paperwork came over, it became clear that I was on the losing end of the deal. I would have also been giving up all the hard work I have into this firm and pride I have by owning a black-owned business. I realized that I would be giving up too soon, and that my breakthrough was on the way!

For every person who has ever sent me a DM, commented, shared my post, called/texted, shared words of encouragement, or told me I inspire them… you all have played a huge role in me keeping this business going. God knows, I face a new challenge almost every day. You all help give me the energy I need to keep pushing and not give up.

> *There is no such thing as an overnight success. However, one day you will wake up and the world will see the fruits of your labor from all the years before.*

Twas Real (Estate) Love

I have been blessed to meet an amazing partner who has completely reinvigorated my view on marriage, love, relationships, friendships, etc. AKB has played a vital role in my life during the past few years. Real estate is what connected us, and genuine love and support is what keeps us together. He has watched me go through the ups and downs of being a business owner. He has had to bear the burden of my down days, or days when I was too busy for him, or days when I must turn down date nights for work nights.

Yet, he has supported me both physically, mentally, financially, and spiritually with every serious idea that I have ever told him about. Thank you for praying over me daily and showing me what it is like to have a partner who genuinely cares about my success. Thank you for being my rock, my friend, and hands down, the absolute best man ever! I look forward to all the things we will continue to build together. I love you, AKB!

If you are dating or married and you want to do business with your partner, I do not think there is anything wrong with it. If you both have skill sets that complement each other, then it could help you both build an empire more quickly.

However, make sure that you are protecting both of your interests and have proper documentation in place.

Marketing Matters

I get so many compliments about my brand, so I
would like to give you guys a little more insight into
how it all came to life. My last name is Williams, but I
did not want to exclude others who choose to work
with me; hence, Williams & Co. I also know that one
of the largest real estate firms in the world uses the
same last name, so I figured if anyone looked them
up, I could potentially come up as an option based on
their SEO. The word international was added
because I have an MBA in International Business. I
also do not think small; I will buy and sell real estate
properties overseas for personal use and for my
clients. Atlanta is a melting pot of many nationalities,
and I want to position my company to provide real
estate services to anyone.

I chose my company colors because I wanted to use colors that would be classic and timeless. I did not want people to be able to determine what race or gender the owner was simply by looking at the brand alone. I wanted colors that were neutral, yet powerful, so I chose the colors navy, gold, and white. Once I selected the name and the colors, I worked closely with a friend/graphic designer to collaborate and bring this dynamic brand to life.

Initially, I could only afford to invest very little into my marketing efforts. I tried to market by using every free method possible to save on overhead expenses. It was not until I really started to understand the importance of investing into my marketing efforts that my business grew substantially! If you are an entrepreneur or an aspiring entrepreneur, I want you to share five particularly important things to remember regarding marketing and branding:

1. If you do not market your business on social media in today's world, you are leaving money on the table.
2. Identify & define your Unique Selling Proposition (USP) upfront so you know exactly what makes you stand out against your competitors.

3. Take a percentage of your monthly income every month and reinvest it into a unique marketing campaign.
4. Be a walking, talking billboard for your brand daily because if you do not believe in your brand, no one else will.
5. Hire a marketing agency if you do not have the time to market or do not know where to start.

If you do not market your business consistently, you are setting up your business to fail. There is no way around it.

Final Thoughts

As you have seen throughout this book, I have experienced the highs and the lows of life both personally and professionally. Every life lesson has played a major role in making me the woman I am today.

No matter how hard it gets, there is nothing like having your own business. I am enormously proud of my brand and the team I have built. I have full creative control of my brand, policies and procedures, company culture, etc. I appreciate every agent who has been a part of my vision and has helped me to grow my brand to what it is today! I cannot take all the credit! There have been some amazing people behind the scenes who have made sacrifices in their lives to support my dreams. I love you all from the bottom of my heart!

I will never forget where I came from. I will always be a little country black girl from Hinesville, GA, who pursued a better life! I cannot wait to bless others around me for the things they have done for me. I do not work this hard simply to have material things or to boast or brag… I work this hard to change the narrative for the generations that will follow me.

So many people say they want to leave a legacy, but they have not laid the first brick in the foundation. There are levels to success. Your journey is not my journey and my pace is not your pace, but one thing we all must remember is that failure is a choice: you can choose to win or you can choose to lose in this life. Choose to win and do not settle for mediocrity.

I will close with this: Never leave your dreams locked away in your mind… bring them forth… fight! Stick with it until you see the fruits of your labor manifest before your eyes! Do not let the Pain, Pitfalls, and Poverty Mindset stop you from getting to Profit, Power, and Prosperity!

Thank you tremendously for your support! If you enjoyed it, please write a review on my website www.DeniseTheBroker.com!

RESOURCES

Denise Williams
Visit: www.DeniseTheBroker.com to enroll in my real estate courses, purchase merchandise, schedule business consultations or homebuyer consultations, etc.
Email: Denise@DeniseTheBroker.com

Connect with Me On Social Media
IG: @denisethebroker
FB: DeniseTheBroker
LinkedIn: Denise Williams
YouTube: DeniseTheBroker

Williams & Co International Realty
Visit www.WilliamsAndCoRealty.com to check out the team, view testimonials, and write a five-star review!
Email: Info@WilliamsAndCoRealty.com

Connect with Us On Social Media
IG: @williamsandcorealty
FB: Williams & Co International Realty
LinkedIn: Williams & Co International Realty
YouTube: Williams & Co International Realty

JANUARY

Write Down Your Goals. Be Specific.

1. _____

_____

_____

2. _____

_____

_____

3. _____

_____

_____

4. _____

_____

_____

5. _____

_____

_____

FEBRUARY

Write Down Your Goals. Be Specific.

1. _____

_____

_____

2. _____

_____

_____

3. _____

_____

_____

4. _____

_____

_____

5. _____

_____

_____

MARCH

Write Down Your Goals. Be Specific.

1. _____

_____

_____

2. _____

_____

_____

3. _____

_____

_____

4. _____

_____

_____

5. _____

_____

_____

APRIL

Write Down Your Goals. Be Specific.

1. _____

_____

_____

2. _____

_____

_____

3. _____

_____

_____

4. _____

_____

_____

5. _____

_____

_____

MAY

Write Down Your Goals. Be Specific.

1. _____

_____

_____

2. _____

_____

_____

3. _____

_____

_____

4. _____

_____

_____

5. _____

_____

_____

JUNE

Write Down Your Goals. Be Specific.

1. _____

_____

_____

2. _____

_____

_____

3. _____

_____

_____

4. _____

_____

_____

5. _____

_____

_____

JULY

Write Down Your Goals. Be Specific.

1. _____

    _____

    _____

2. _____

    _____

    _____

3. _____

    _____

    _____

4. _____

    _____

    _____

5. _____

    _____

    _____

AUGUST

Write Down Your Goals. Be Specific.

1. _____

   _____

   _____

2. _____

   _____

   _____

3. _____

   _____

   _____

4. _____

   _____

   _____

5. _____

   _____

   _____

SEPTEMBER

Write Down Your Goals. Be Specific.

1. _____

_____

_____

2. _____

_____

_____

3. _____

_____

_____

4. _____

_____

_____

5. _____

_____

_____

OCTOBER

Write Down Your Goals. Be Specific.

1. _____

   _____

   _____

2. _____

   _____

   _____

3. _____

   _____

   _____

4. _____

   _____

   _____

5. _____

   _____

   _____

NOVEMBER

Write Down Your Goals. Be Specific.

1. _____

_____

_____

2. _____

_____

_____

3. _____

_____

_____

4. _____

_____

_____

5. _____

_____

_____

DECEMBER

Write Down Your Goals. Be Specific.

1. _____
   _____
   _____

2. _____
   _____
   _____

3. _____
   _____
   _____

4. _____
   _____
   _____

5. _____
   _____
   _____

WORDS OF AFFIRMATION

I AM CONFIDENT IN MY ABILITY TO BE

SUCCESSFUL

MONEY FLOWS TO ME FROM BOTH

EXPECTED AND UNEXPECTED SOURCES

I MAKE A DIFFERENCE IN THE WORLD

I WILL NOT COMPARE MYSELF TO

OTHERS ON THE INTERNET

I OVERCOME FEARS AND FOLLOW MY

DREAMS

EVEN IF I DIDN'T COME FROM A RICH FAMILY, A RICH FAMILY CAN COME FROM ME

I HAVE A HEALTHY BODY, VIBRANT

SOUL AND TRANQUIL MIND

THERE IS NO LIMIT ON MY POTENTIAL

I HAVE A FORGIVING HEART

I ATTRACT MONEY EASILY INTO MY

LIFE

I AM WORTHY OF LOVE AND

HAPPINESS

I AM NOT THE SUM OF MY MISTAKES

I AM ALWAYS IN MY DEFINING

MOMENT

I AM THE MAINIFESTATION OF MY

FAMILY'S PRAYERS

I GIVE MYSELF THE ATTENTION AND

CARE THAT I DESERVE

I AM UNIQUE AND HIGHLY FAVORED

I AM A CONDUIT OF ALL THINGS GOOD; I ATTRACT GOODNESS, IT FLOWS THROUGH ME, AND IT BLESSES THE WORLD

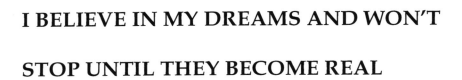

I BELIEVE IN MY DREAMS AND WON'T

STOP UNTIL THEY BECOME REAL

I DON'T ENTERTAIN NEGATIVITY IN

ANY SHAPE OR FORM

FAILURE IS NEVER AN OPTION

EXCUSES ARE NOT A PART OF MY
VOCABULARY. I MAKE THINGS
HAPPEN.

I DON'T WAIT FOR OPPORTUNITIES. I CREATE THEM.

I HOPE THIS BOOK WAS A BLESSING TO
YOU!

THANK YOU AGAIN FOR YOUR
SUPPORT!

Made in the USA
Columbia, SC
15 August 2023

21590345R00061